PRICE RIGHT

Then sell.

Graeme Smith

PUBLISHED ON AMAZON.com
by
LABYRINTH BOOKS

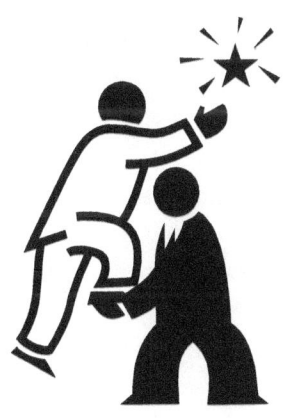

DEDICATION:

This book is dedicated to my family.

Hele-ly (Ly).
        my wife:

Ingrid.
        our daughter:

Marie.
        my former wife:

Fiona, Natalie and Michael
        our children:

Georgie
        Michael's wife:

Pearl, Kiki and Martha.
        their children:

They have had to put up with me for many years and I thank them for that.
I hope this book gives them an insight into what has occupied me.
All have done worthwhile and interesting things in the absence of my help.
I congratulate them for their achievements.

HOW TO USE THIS BOOK.

First think - then do.
Usually people don't think through things to the level they need to.
Because of that, they have projects instead of tasks on their "to do" list.
That leads to procrastination as it hasn't been broken down to a task level.

So go through your book once to understand it.
Go through it again.

Then start at the idea you would like to implement first.
Make notes of the steps you will need to take and the resources required.
Use these notes to create a step by step system for implementing the guide.
Often you will not refer to the original, once you've created **YOUR** system.

The first question to ask and answer is "Why is this being done?"
How does this align with where you want to get to?
What are the strategic implications of doing this?
Does this fit with getting to your goal in the shortest and fastest time?
What would it be like if it were totally successful?
Define it - what is success for this project and how will you know?

Now brainstorm all the tasks that are involved in your project.
It's important not to go linear too fast with this.
By linear, I mean step one, step two, step three, and step four.
You end up cutting off options.
As you plan step one, two, three, there is a specific step that might be four.
Start steps too quickly, other ways for one, two and three may not appear.

The first third of any brainstorming session is really easy.
Just come up with lots of ideas.
The second third is challenging - go through ideas and see where they lead.
Then push yourself to think a little bit outside the box.
That's often where the big idea is!
That's where the most powerful way of getting a project done fastest - is.

Most people never get to that level and short-change themselves.
Then their project takes longer and they also set up to procrastinate.
This final brainstorming part of the equation is incredibly important.

Once fully brainstormed put your options into a linear sequence.
Then you can figure out what you've overlooked.
Everything becomes obvious as you get your tasks in order.
Now add missing steps and you have laid out your task list for this project.

When you've organized the tasks into a linear process decide:
What things can you start immediately?
What can be started that are not dependent on what occurred before them?
Obviously that is step one.
There might be step five, six or twenty that don't rely on anything else to do.
You can get started on them right away too.

Now use a folder.
Write things you think of at the time and also cross off things as you do them.
Add in stuff that is relevant from time to time.

PRICE RIGHT.

INDEX: PRICE RIGHT

SUPPORT:

The Australian Artist magazine – magazine for artists

The International Artist magazine – magazine for artists

Clipping Path Universe – for photo-shop editing

Cherri Computers – computer hardware, software and printers

1. SUPPLY and DEMAND.

Reviewed by Susan Curtin - (Cambewarra Village, Australia).
1. Understanding supply and demand.
2. Professional artists must sell artworks.
3. Are there price guides?
4. Are you a major artist, well established and selling well?
5. **There's another way!**

1. Understanding supply and demand!

Fortunes from the spice trade inspired great discovery voyages.
Pepper was worth its weight in gold in those days.
It was also very scarce.
All commerce is based on the laws of supply and demand.

If something is scarce and demand high, people pay a premium price.
As they did for spices.

But the more there is of something the less demand there is likely.
The price is correspondingly lower.

Demand is more important than supply in determining price.
Now let's look at the art market in relation to supply and demand.

Basically there's a huge supply of artworks (of whatever standard).
Art is more popular than ever before.
People are attending classes and more people are painting regularly.
Those who have been doing it for years just keep on painting.

On the other hand, demand is not even close to matching this supply.
There are many stories of art shows where only a few paintings sold.
Exhibitions in galleries with the same result.
And artists who have studios bursting with unsold paintings.
There are exceptions of course, but really it's always been like that!

If no-one wants your paintings then you can't sell them!
It will not matter how many you have.

In the overall picture, demand for artworks has never matched supply.
That's why the majority of artworks are never sold, but gather dust.
We are operating in a depressed industry.

Demand for some individual artists exceeds the supply of their works.
Those artists have been successful.
Therein is the hope that inspires all but for most artists the reality is different.

The market has shrunk even more in recent years.
Money previously spent on things like artworks has been diverted.
Superannuation funds, shares, various other forms of financial investments.
Many people have less money to spend as taxation is more efficient.
The art market has shrunk most at the level most artists are operating at.
High priced works still sell (say $10,000 +).
There are always rich people, no matter what the economic circumstances.
Luxury cars have still been selling for example.

If price is high then not as many sales are needed to maintain income.
That's why you, or any artist, should aim up market, for sales are still there.
This is not an easy task for someone at the beginning of his or her career.
Yet it should be an integral part of your career plan.
Does your career plan have strategies for increasing demand for your work?
If so you can develop plans for increasing your prices as well.
An aspiring professional, and any artist in a new venue, should start low.
But that isn't where you want to stay.

Most artists may be tempted to reduce prices from time to time.
Sometimes you have to do that as a part of re-evaluating a stagnant career!
This doesn't always increase chances of a sale, unless the reduction is great.
Then you must sell more for the same return as in the past.
These days that's unlikely.

Instead of reducing price, paint better and increase price.
Lowering prices and discounting is dealt with more fully later in this book.
Also for the same reasons a lower priced gallery is also likely to go under.

2. Professional artists must sell artworks.

With no clients and prospects it isn't possible for a professional career.
It will not matter how well you paint!
Pricing has a great deal of influence on whether a sale takes place.
Pricing policy and consequent sales are related to the income you enjoy.

Are you in business, have a career, or in a profession?
Then money is a measure of how well you do.
It's not the motivation, that's your desire to follow your dream.
But your income says something about how well you've followed that dream.
Money also makes achieving your dream more feasible.
It's likely more income links to a better lifestyle.
You can live in a garret in poverty or have the lifestyle you'd like.
Either way your work will remain of much the same standard.

Do you like selling?
What happens to your unsold works?
Can you pay someone else to sell for you?
What will happen if you don't sell your works?
Do you have a problem being more assertive?
What will happen if you don't improve?

Compare these approaches?
A work for $500 with an add value item costing $25 but is worth $50.
New value to buyer is $550 but the new cost to you is old cost + $25.
If the same work is discounted by $25.
The value to buyer is still $500 BUT the new cost to you is old cost + $25.

Which approach is more likely to sell?
What if the add value cost to you was nothing at all (copyright)?
You can see which way to go can't you?
What is the cost of doing nothing in $$$?
What is the cost of doing nothing in other ways?

Price is an important factor in determining if a sale will take place.
It's not the most important though as many artists believe to be the case.
If prospects don' like your work it will not usually matter what the price is.
If they like your work then price can assist towards or be a barrier to a sale.

In real estate buyers usually spend 10% to 15% more than they intend.
Many owners put 10% to 15% on top of the price they hope to attain.
There's a 20% to 30% gap between advertised price and likely buyer price.

Overcoming that gap requires the negotiating skill of the agent.
If the price of a property is too high buyers are lost, they don't look.
If the property is too low then the chance to attain a premium price is lost.
At an auction there is a different scenario as the price is unknown.
So what about marketing a property (or painting) without a stated price?
I've done this in my gallery owning days and found it to be well worthwhile.
It's what actually happens at auctions.

We had a price but it was not displayed and was varied if necessary.
An advantage is you attract all interested people whatever they will pay.
Price is no longer a barrier.
No price is a problem for those who are curious but have no intention to buy.
But such people should not be given any more than polite time.

The work is judged on its features and how they benefit a prospect.
A listed price no longer acts as an impediment to attracting buyers.
The chances of underselling are removed completely.
Opportunities for a premium price remain as no actual buyer is eliminated.

The most luxurious vehicles for sale usually display $POA as the price,
Maybe your works could also be $POA?

Have you tried not advertising prices of your works?
Try it for a month and see what happens.

3. Are there price guides?

Beginning professionals can guess and hope to get it roughly right.
Fortunately there are some signposts for guidance.

Compare outlets, and potential outlets, for your work.
Try to take advantage of their business strengths.
Some galleries sell many etchings for example, whereas others none.
It's obvious the 'etching' galleries may not be major outlets for oil paintings.
But they might sell your drawings.

Look at where you have your work for sale, or hope to.
What sorts of prices are actually obtained for works by other artists there?
Try to find work roughly comparable with your own.
See how they're actually selling.
Ask the owner, sales people, etc.
What size are the ones that sell, not necessarily those on the wall.
Now you have an idea of how to commence pricing in that place.
It could be different in other venues.

Find out the status of an artist with works are comparable to your own.
Are they popular in that particular gallery, art show or other venue?
Perhaps they're generally well known in the art world?
If this is the case you won't be able to command the same prices.
Even if you believe your work to be superior you'll have to accept less.

Talk to each gallery owner, about their business.
Don't say 'What sells here?' even though this is something you want to know.
Ask what their exhibition policies are.
How do they approach pricing?
Who are their major artists?

Eventually you could have different prices for different outlets.
Many artists believe the opposite, it's actually quite a reasonable thing to do.
Supply different works to different places according to client buying patterns.
At Gallery XYZ in New York you could have the most expensive works.
In a picture framer's sales area in a suburb of a city modestly priced prints.

Price according to what the buyer has to pay.
It is this price that determines whether the buyer will buy or not.
They do not know what sort of commission arrangements you have.
And don't care either and it's actually none of the buyer's business.

Commission rates are a common business arrangement.
But you should NOT price according to the commission structure.
Usually the galleries with the highest commission rates also sell best.
They sell for higher prices too so you get higher prices in these galleries.
Your return is better than at a poor selling outlet with a low commission rate.
Basically 0% of $0 is nothing, whereas 90% of $something is still something.

It's the total dollar return that's most important to you.
A commission rate is important in helping you calculate your likely income.
Deduct commission from the selling price calculate a cost or wholesale price.
Might be important to decide which works to allocate to a particular gallery.

4. Are you a major artist, well established and selling well?

There's no real problem just business as usual - well not quite.
If you've not exhibited there before you may not be well-known.
Their most popular artists may be people they've never heard of before too.
You may need price as a strategy to penetrate the new market for your work.

Could you use incentives?
Perhaps you could supply some small prints, which are cheaper?
Older works which have not sold at their regular outlets could be supplied?
They now could be at a lower than usual price as well.
Let's face it, you are running out of opportunities to sell these works.
A new outlet can be a way of clearing old stock to get something for them.

The main aim though is become established in the new outlet.
It's easier said than done but once you succeed, prices can rise (gradually).
Eventually they are at whatever level the market will bear.

An initial strategy, for established artists or starters in the art business.
Price at less than the competition in a new outlet.
It may be the established artist has no competition.
Even so it's worthwhile to hold a small carrot out to initial buyers.
They will talk their friends into buying their work, so they should be rewarded.
But as you become established put prices up as part of a planned process.

If you recently entered professional ranks, a low start price is critical.
Being completely unknown you do everything to overcome this disadvantage.
Your starting price when linked to few sales won't be economically sensible.
But it costs money to get established in any business including an artist!
Let's think about car manufacturers for a moment.
Car makers have been in business for some time and it costs megabucks.
What do they do when they launch a new model or penetrate a new market?
Special deals for early buyers who provide exposure in its intended market.
This will include celebrities and sportspeople (but not artists yet).

Selling paintings is no different.
It's still people who do the buying.
Your works should be where they're supposed to be, on people's walls.
The quicker this happens, the better.

A low entry level price is uneconomic but essential for long term sales.
The importance of long-term thinking should not be under-estimated.

5. There's another way!

If we increase a client's perception of value they will pay a higher price.
AND the more readily they'll pay it.
New cars have extras at prices less than normally paid - you do the same.

As already mentioned, each buyer determines value for himself.
But there's no question a buyer's notion of value can be changed.
You and your gallery, must change buyers' ideas about value.
Particularly over the longer term.
In general, price work as low as you can possibly bear to start with.
It's more important to cultivate dealer, gallery and client relationships.
Than to sell just one work.

Ignore those who say you should never lower your prices.
Art prices fluctuate just like real estate and the stock market.
Low prices will attract interest and encourage people to take a risk on you.
This is better than having a painting sitting unsold in your studio.

Maybe this experiment will help as you are just starting out.
Pretend a prospect has come to your studio and seen a work they like.
The price of this work is usually $750 and they offer you $10 for it.
Would you be willing to sell it for that price - what if the offer was $5000?
Between $10 and $5000 there is a price at which you are prepared to sell.
You may not be totally happy and feel the painting is worth more.
But it is the lowest possible price you can live with and now, double it.

You now have a retail price and a wholesale price for that work.
That's if a gallery or agent takes 50% commission of a sale they make.
This price remains steady until you experience one or more of the following:
Increased sales,
Increases in the number of exhibitions you participate in,
Increase in the number galleries that represent you,
There is an inflationary effect.

But it can go up or down.
If there is a decrease in those factors consider a reduction in price!
Do not be in a hurry to make any changes though.
To price other work, adjust according to size, subject matter and medium.
Eventually your price is decided by the market and what people actually pay.
If you sell a lot, then perhaps your prices are too low.
But if you are not selling at all then they need to be lower.

Remember, this is just a starting point.
If you have a gallery representative, they should work with you.
They can help you determine a realistic price for you work.

Should you focus on selling price or cost price?
It's money in your bank that is your major concern.
So cost price should be your focus.
It doesn't matter if one person sells your work and makes more than another.
Just as long as sales take place and you receive what you want is important.

What about if you have to sell the work yourself?
Well the best people to ask are your potential clients!
Have a small function, and invite a number of potential buyers (say 10 or 12).
Have some eats and drinks.
Tell them you want to do some market research to help your career.
Show them some of your works one at a time.
Select typical works in your usual range of sizes.

Ask them to write down what they think each work would sell for.
Also ask them would they be likely to buy works such as these.
Ask how much they'd pay (which could be different).
Ask any other questions you want answers to.
Collect the answers and then have a general discussion.

Price testing is the way to determine what price gives the best return.
This issue will be dealt with more fully in a later chapter.

2. PRICING.

1. In spite of a widely held belief your artwork doesn't sell itself.

If it did, you'd be able to hang a work anywhere and people would buy.
There should be a correlation between what you do, where and how it's sold.

Selling is helping people buy.
When people buy you can make money!
There are three main ways to do this.

1. Get more clients and this is what most artists focus on.
So it's likely to be the first thing you probably want to do - get more clients.

2. Sell more stuff to existing clients.
Few people ever really take this step.
The focus is usually on getting more first up (front-end) clients.
BUT there's a goldmine waiting in your current client database.

3. You can also have clients increase the frequency of their purchases.
That's the third way to get more money - sell clients more stuff **more often.**
Create more stuff and offer that to your clients on a regular scheduled basis.

Note the words "regular" and "scheduled".
The best way is to actually plan your new works for a year in advance.
Even to the extent of releasing something new every month.
If you're putting good stuff out, your clients are waiting for something new.

They'll want you to hurry up and come out with another new work!
Most artists think they'll saturate the market **BUT** it just **DOESN'T** happen!
Didn't happen to Picasso, did it?

Now you have the three main strategies to make you money.

2. How can you increase the size of each transaction!

Simply charge more.
This is an easy way to get more money instead of new, exciting, hard ways.
Here is an old, proven, and easy way to get more money **RIGHT NOW**.

There is one main reason you should not be afraid to charge more.
People actually believe if it costs more money it is better.
People automatically desire the more expensive option.
Even if they don't buy it because they don't have the money.
They still want it just so they can have it and feel special.
Wanting the most expensive thing is common behaviour.

Think about golf shirts.
There's absolutely no difference between a Polo golf shirt and others.
Except the Polo label and the fact that it is more expensive.
Why do people still think, "Oh, Polo is better."?

Because it's more expensive, that's why.
There is scientific research into a correlation of wine prices and quality.
This research supports the notion that price determines quality.

In art it is no different.
In his day van Gogh's paintings were thought inferior – he couldn't sell any.
What about now - have the paintings changed?

Charging more obviously help you increase the size of a transaction.
What if you're afraid to just charge more for the sake of charging more?
You could build more value into the sale.

What if you're selling a print?
Add an audio component and charge more for your advanced audio bundle.
Add a screen cam video, charge more as you've added value (video edition!)
Go from a print to the original painting and charge much more.

Another thing you can do is add bonuses.
You lift the price because the perceived value of your overall offer is better.
An invitation to visit your studio is worth quite a bit extra for example.

Charge more by adding scarcity and exclusiveness.
Only allow 5 people to take your painting course and it's very expensive too.
BUT those 5 people are going to get more personal interaction with you.
Instant price justification.

Offer a deluxe version and increase the transaction.
If you paint in standard sizes (you should) offer a standard but basic frame.
The deluxe version has a much better frame with a special label with a title.

After an initial purchase sell a deluxe version as a never repeated offer
They buy a painting and you say "Wait, I'll only make this offer one time".
For an additional $47 dollars you can now have the deluxe version."
You see this all the time because **IT WORKS**.

3. You can also sell them more stuff!

Increase the amount of times people buy stuff from you.
You need back end products to sell.
That could be sell other works to existing clients.

If they bought once they'll probably buy often if you have good stuff.
Then you can increase the size of your transactions on the back end.
Which means you sell more and more expensive stuff on the back end.

What should you offer on the back-end?
The fastest way to create a back end is develop a gold edition.
Offer that to existing clients and also as an up-sell to all new clients.
This may involve paring down the original basic product concurrently.

If you develop those sales from front end sales then clients will buy.
You could start with prints or small works and build up to expensive originals.
Also **SELL** a studio inspection tour for a little bit or a lot, whatever you want.
Another immediate thing you can do on the back end is to sell live events.
For example, if you sell oil paintings sell lessons on how to paint skies in oils.

You can also sell seminars.
Plan your career to sell quarterly seminars.
The seminars could be: hanging paintings, frame design, matching curtains.
If you sell a seminar to your clients and are worried nobody is going to come.
Stop worrying.
People want to be around other people like themselves – they'll come.

This is the ladder theory.
If you place a ladder in front of somebody they want to climb it.
If you know that there's another level you could be at you want to get there.
Create gold, platinum, titanium, elite, inside-circle levels for people to join.
More expensive platinum, deluxe, deluxe, exclusive products people buy.
They'll buy them **BUT** you **MUST** deliver massive value.

Then you will create an increased frequency of purchase.
A one-time buyer now buys something else from you.
For all future clients the size of the transactions is increased.
They can give you more money for the gold edition of what you're selling.
That's why it pays to have small and cheap works for sale (even prints).
They're front-end for back-end sales of larger original works at higher prices.

Price qualifies your prospects more than you might realize.
We've always been taught "You get what you pay for".
Price sets up expectations for **PRICE IS** the guide to **QUALITY**.

BUT you can deliver more value too:
Ultimately the value provided dictates the profit you receive from prospects.
Increase the value and your income goes up.
High-profit products with high-margins have more room for sensational value.
You can throw in high-value extras!
In addition you can afford truly unique unadvertised bonuses and follow-ups.
Your back-end products or services should be high value AND high priced!

You will OWN the marketplace if your work has a premium price:
You can spend more on advertising, testing unusual advertising places, etc.
You can also afford to pay more to acquire a prospect.
The prospect is a better prospect and you can make bad results work too.
High-price products only need small % response low-price to make money.
That applies to artists as well!

Most people undercharge for what they provide.
If your stuff isn't good enough for you to raise the price on it – make it better!
Making it cheaper will not work!

4. How important is size?

Is there a correlation between size and cost?
Most beginning artists are aware of a relationship between size and cost.
That's why they usually paint small paintings.
Often their teachers exhort them to work larger and 'free up'.

It's difficult to 'free up' if you're worried about the cost of the materials.
The most obvious costs are frames, stretchers, canvas or paper, and paint.
But there's also the cost in time.

Bigger works also take far longer to complete than small ones.
This leads to a productivity cost.
In a given time more small works can be produced than larger ones.
For a beginner it's a better pathway to "free up" than few larger works.

Is there value in smaller works?
A small work doesn't cost too much to frame, even elaborately.
However, the frame cost proportion of any selling price is quite high.
This reduces considerably the return on small works.
It can make selling small works uneconomical, except in very high volumes.
But that is difficult for a fledgling artist to achieve anyway.

What is done depends on time / cost related to quicker production.
There's still value in small works, even if frames are major inroads to return.
Small paintings can be used to open up a market for your work.
Once that has been done the size and prices can be increased.
Then you start to reap a better reward for your efforts.

Can you control the size of a work?
If you can you control the major costs of production (as distinct from selling).
Ability to control size of works distinguishes professional from leisure artists.
It's actually quite easy.
Just control the size of canvas, paper, board, plate or surface you work on.
That determines the size of your work before you even start!

Similar sized works and you can make cost effective framing choices.
Quite obviously you can re-use frames.
If you paint to a standard size, then all of your works will be that size.
They fit the same size frame and you don't have to frame them all, just some.
Works can be swapped in frames, with more frames made as sales happen.
Thus ten works may only cost you three or four frames to start with.

A development is to standardize the sizes of your frames.
I have four major frame sizes, each of which is ½ or 2x the size of another.
Occasionally I paint an even larger work, which is still in the same proportion.
I don't have many spare frames, although I have unsold work (unframed).

If some works are the same size, only a few actually need framing.
The works can be rotated in the frames from time to time.

Then it is possible to provide unframed works to galleries.
Supply fewer frames so they swap them as they show your work to clients.
This way a gallery can have a good supply of your paintings.
But you don't have to spend too much on framing (or freight).

After a while you can even standardize frame styles.
You'll discover which frames look the best and sell the best too.
Then your works are in a number of places, presented well in optimum sizes.
But they haven't cost you any more than necessary for framing.

Control the size of your works then you can also control prices.

5. Artists usually relate their prices to different sizes.

It's also happens in most other fields.
You pay more for a large car by the same manufacturer, than a smaller one.
A big house is always more than a small similar standard one.
So it is for artwork.
It's also what people expect.
An aspiring or professional artist should produce all works up to a standard.
The only real difference is size.

What about the lesser works you may say?
Works that are not to your usual standard (some) should be destroyed.
Cut them down, paint them over, or otherwise make them disappear.
Do not put inferior works on sale at any price!
You will regret it down the track if you do not take this seemingly drastic step.
Don't give them away for some "good' works will come back to haunt you.

Well what about the really good works you may now say?
There will always be some paintings you prefer over others.
But other people's choices will usually be different.
If this wasn't the case, you'd only sell the works you really like!

People buy what they like, not what you like.
Price it (or them) the same as other works the same size.
Otherwise do not offer them for sale - keep and enjoy these works yourself.

It's hard for a gallery to sell if there's no correlation in price and size.
This is particularly so at higher price levels.
The artist sends signals the work is not consistent and quality varies.
Some of my works are better than others **BUT** do you really want to do that?

People are confused if their choice is at a lower price than it should be.
They tend to back off.
So check your works for their quality and remove those not up to the mark.
Which means the others can be priced according to sizes (and media also).

Another important consideration is the number of sizes you work in.
Perhaps three or four different sizes could be enough.
Size variations linked to price difference is important to marketing effectively.
With variations you can adjust prices without people being aware.

3. SELL FOR LOWER PRICES AND SELL MORE.

Reviewed by Monik Robichaud - (West Kelowna - Canada)

1. Live by price then possibly die by price!
2. How do price and discounts relate?
3. Why are discounts everywhere?
4. How do you maintain value?
5. The strategy is price change.

1. Live by price then possibly die by price!

Out in the real world, there are businesses that live and die on price.
They're always having sales, discounts, special promotions and so on.
No matter where you live, you'll know them.
Hardware stores, clothing shops, furniture places, and grocery chains.
Price is the basis of their appeal to clients and thus their operation.
You'd have to be blind not to know of the pressure to sell at lower prices.

There are not so many artists who do this.
We tend to have our own particular approach to price, which is the opposite.
We'll never drop our prices for we stay loyal to previous buyers.
Even if there are no sales and we're in grave danger of starving.
But do they stay loyal to you?

So these days there's a great deal of pressure to give discounts.
It's not generally a good idea, as your return is reduced.
There's no increase in turnover to compensate, as with other retailers.

If you give a discount there MUST be reason, other than someone asks.
What will they give you in return for the discount?
What reduction will they accept for the discount (no frame, no copyright)?
Do they want a best work or one you've had for years with no interest?
Strike a deal that makes you happy, or walk away from it.

But you must sell more to earn the same amount as previously.
Sometimes this is possible, but only for the biggest of businesses.
The rest, including us, sell much the same amount, and make less money.
Now that's not a very smart thing to do, because that's how you die by price.

Do clients buy on the basis of price, ever?
If you have no money, there's little alternative but to consider the price.
But even then, a poor person does not ever buy what they don't need.
Others might think they don't need whatever it was but a buyer never does.

If someone is thinking of buying a work and you lowered the price.
It may be sufficient to capture a sale.
On the other hand you may have made the sale anyway but you never know.

But what if someone wasn't contemplating such a purchase?
Then even a major reduction is unlikely to make any difference.
Clients buy what's in it for them so a work has to do something they want.
Selling a car is easier than selling a painting for this reason.
A car allows mobility, prestige, safety, status, economy, trade-in old car, etc.
There are many reasons why a car can help the buyer do something.
But your painting can do some of those things too (prestige, status).
So perhaps art isn't so hard to sell after all, only when done the wrong way.

Is there a difference between a benefit and price?
Understand the distinction of benefits to the prospect and price you charge.
Then you'll also start to realize how this makes a major difference to sales.
Increase the gap between benefit and price, make your work more attractive.
Keep your price at the premium end of the market.
Still offer good value with extra benefits which don't cost anything (prestige).

Reducing price reduces profit by the same amount (costs same).
Don't fall into a discount trap to make an offer more attractive (cheapens).
Make your business more profitable by adding benefits to justify higher price.
Never respond directly to a price question but probe for the facts.
What would your reaction be if I said (whatever)?

Clients buy to solve a problem.
But why should a prospect buy from you rather than anyone else?
The more distinguishable you are in the mind of a prospect.
The more you stand out from any opposition you might have.
Eventually you may stand alone, without any opposition at all!

How can you back this up?
The most effective tool is a risk-reversal policy (a guarantee).
It moves risk from the buyer to you, so it is easier for a prospect to say 'yes'.
Your guarantee should appeal to 98% decent people.
Don't worry about the other 2%.

2. How do price and discounts relate?

When you start out on a professional art career, pricing is a mystery.
Discounting is another mystery and obviously it's related to pricing.

If you intend to discount then what's the first pricing decision?
Make sure your pricing has a margin built in, so you can.
In other words one of the first pricing decisions is, whether or not to discount.

Learn from Asian traders who know they'll be bargaining for a sale.
In other words they're prepared to give discounts.
They also know people with whom they deal have **NO** idea of original cost.
They mark-up sufficiently so even after a discounted sale there's a profit.
To make a sale, it doesn't matter what goods cost, only what someone pays.
To make a profit, there needs to be a margin, obviously the bigger the better.

An artist is in a good position to sell at a discount, if you choose.
Your costs are usually relatively small compared with the likely selling price.
The more successful the artist the greater the margin is likely to be.
Make your margin whatever you like **BUT** make it large if you are to discount.

But will you give discounts?
The capacity to discount is still not the same as actually giving a discount.
Discounting is a two-edged sword.
If you start giving price reductions, you'll have to keep giving them.
At least to the same people, as well as anyone else who knows!
A small discount may be attractive at first, eventually this loses its impact.
You must give larger discounts to make the same sales, at reduced profits.

Public discounting leads to greater difficulty in avoiding this problem.
You can give discounts to favoured buyers at special times more easily.

The key to discounting is that there has to be a genuine reason for it.
For example, it makes sense to discount works you want to get rid of.
They're older works, or a style you no longer do, or not up to your standard.
You could discount these heavily (at least 1/3 off price) just to move them.
There's no sense in discounting your latest, best and most expensive works.

There are other justifications for discounting.
Works have been specially produced, in order to be discounted.
Holding a 'Xmas Xhibition' (see elsewhere) is an example of this approach.
Often prints are produced, to be sold as a cheaper line of artworks.
There may be times when you really need sales, so discounting is used.

In most retail situations, the end of the financial year is such a time.
This could apply if you need to reduce stock to avoid excessive tax liability.

Should you give discounts to certain people?
Well it depends.

It depends on what you get for the discount.
If all you get is less money, there's no reason to discount unless desperate.
In that case, anything is justifiable, as survival is the most important factor.
But even then you could say, OK you can have this work for only $x.
But at that price I'll have to take it out of the frame.

Perhaps a potential buyer has a very well-known art collection.
It could be worth discounting to be included in such a collection.
But only if you intend to publicize the fact as a way to even more sales.
Public galleries in capital and major provincial cities are in this category too.
Other institutions (universities) are worth discounting to for the same reason.

Corporate collections are worth being in if a work is on public display.
Places lacking prestige but show work to large audiences ca be favoured.
In the beginning you'll probably not have too many of these opportunities.
But keep your eye out for them.

What do you do if someone asks for a discount?
First of all you should have a policy, along the lines suggested above.
If I give you a discount, what will you give me?
You can weigh up the answer and if you like what they offer give a discount.
On the other hand the only thing a potential buyer offers is they'll buy.
That's not usually sufficient unless they're in one of the above categories.

Let's say all they are doing, is offering to buy, what do you do next.
Say something along the lines of:
I think carefully about the price on my works and believe they are good value.
Obviously you don't agree with this.
Perhaps that means you don't like my works sufficiently?

Usually the person, who wants a discount, has the money.
A person without sufficient money will ask for time to pay, which is allowed.

3. Why are discounts everywhere?

People are more discerning about how they spend a dollar these days.
They're taking longer to pay for your works than in the past too.
There's probably less spare dollars now than for quite a number of years.
Discounts reduce price to below a buyer's expectation of value.
If people lack money, they have no alternative for quality isn't really an issue.
A discount does give an appearance of higher quality than actually paid for.

There are people who could afford to pay more, but choose not to.
This is their right.
We all spend little on things of low importance and more on things we value.

One reason people respond to discounts is greed.
They think they're obtaining something worth more than they actually pay.
Sometimes that may even be the case.
A starving artist has to sell a major painting to eat but usually it's not like this.
In normal commercial circumstances something is worth what was paid for it.
No more, no less.
The discount price is the real price, it's what the buyer paid and seller got.
It's the economic principle; price is the measure of value.
If you're a seller, as you are, then you should not forget this principle.
You only get what you are paid.

But what is something worth?
People judge the value of something and relate that to how much they'd pay.
Different goods can then be compared on price.
Art lovers do it at art exhibitions for not all paintings are the same price.
Art lovers do not equally like all paintings so a mental balance sheet is made.
The most liked painting is bought if the price is right and money is available.
A discount can make the price right.

We tend to be knowledgeable about some things and less about others.
Thus we believe we can judge quality in some things but not in others.
In the areas where we're confident we'll back our judgment and pay more.
In other areas we tend to rely on price as a guide.
We are vulnerable to discounting in these areas.

Most people aren't knowledgeable about art and only pay low prices.
These people are more likely to respond to discounts.
As sophistication grows so does price paid the need to discount reduces.
Eventually a premium price is paid and there is no suggestion of discounting.

Eventually people assume the price will always be discounted.
Then the real measure of value is the discounted price.
So, not only is the real price reduced but also the perception of real value.
To guard against this there is a justification that doesn't reduce value.
Otherwise no discount.

Discounting reduces price, so you must sell more for same return.
So discounting means less actual money for you and your gallery.
Unless there's a large increase in the volume of sales to compensate.

In the art business it's extremely unlikely to happen.
You'll not only need to sell more, but paint more, which may be a problem.

Most people cannot judge quality.
They assume all artwork in the same price bracket is of equivalent standard.
Discount and that's where the road ends people are used to a lower quality.
A higher standard is unavailable, even for those who want and appreciate it.
Except at very much higher prices!
Our community is the poorer.
Consumer legislation tends to reinforce this trend.
As a basic premise is the consumers 'right' to have the lowest price.

All those imported 'originals' are being bought by someone.
They've made it difficult for local amateurs to sell work, at a similar price.
Mass produced prints are having the same effect.

But let's return to whether there are effective discounts?
Discounts must be large to be effective.
10% gets few people into the shoe store, clothing shop, or wherever.
There must be large mark-ups to start to make 50% off and similar possible.
Price works highly with an intention of discounting or loss to get rid of works.

Perhaps you price highly with the intention of discounting?
People who paid full price are in a difficult place if discounts are announced.
They've been ripped off so soon they don't buy or they wait for the discounts.
Now your price is the discounted price, but at the expense of goodwill.

Why buy at the marked price if you know in the future the price is less?
This is particularly pertinent to artwork which doesn't change with seasons.
There are people who'll wait for years for the right artwork or the right price.

People seeking discounts say the price is more than they will pay.
They assume all sellers have sufficient margins to be able to drop the price.
With the size of discounts advertised, it's obvious many can.
Widespread discounting means bargaining is common for buyers and sellers.

Set what you believe to be a reasonable price to start with.
Then why should someone get a discount just because they ask for it?
What about those people who didn't ask?
Perhaps one of them would have bought at the lower discounted price?
But only if they'd have known!

There's no reason to give people discounts just because they ask.
Ask them what they're going to do to justify receiving the discount.
If you give a discount make sure you get something, over and above a sale.

A simple illustration is to sell copyright with the work.
You receive a bonus of your choice (+10%) and a buyer gets something too.
It's a win/win situation which is the ideal to strive for in any selling situation.

4. How do you maintain value?

In art it's pretty obvious there is an over-supply of artworks.
Unsold works, in studios, galleries, is the amount supply exceeds demand.
Any industry where supply exceeds demand is a depressed industry.
This is as true for the art industry as it is for wool, car, or housing industries.

You need to know and understand that this is the situation.
That's the first step towards a realistic appraisal of what is possible.
Then you can be a serious participant in the art industry, as an artist.

It's not usually sufficient that you be a 'good' artist.
Many very talented people do not 'make it'.
Many do of course.

What's the difference between the successful and those who aren't?
If it's not about being a 'good' artist then what is it about?
It **IS** about making the best of whatever artist you are, in an economic sense.
It's a tough business!
Intelligent planning, courage, determination and persistence, it is possible.

You must be careful to guard client perception of value of your works.
It's a perception that is very fragile and easily damaged.
Each of your works is something like pieces of a porcelain tea set.
Once one piece is damaged; the set is lessened in value.
I'm not talking about actual physical damage but perceived value damage.

One work can reduce the value of all works.
If the client's perception is changed sufficiently.
Be constantly be on your guard; to maintain a high value perception.

Insist at all people who handle your works wear cotton gloves.
That's pretty unusual, but all public gallery employees wear cotton gloves.
So why not commercial galleries, and even, or more so art show organizers?

This tells people you value your works and they should too.
This message is also conveyed to their (and your) clients.
OK that's one way you can convey an appreciation of value for your works.
They warrant museum like handling, and they're precious.
Naturally you and your agent wear white gloves when handling your work.

Now what about if one of your galleries doesn't do this?
Not a problem if they're thousands of miles from the nearest other outlet.
What if they are closer, a hundred miles or another suburb in the same city?
Still no problem you might say!

What if one of your buyers visits several galleries, as many do?
They come across one not handling your work in the appropriate manner.
What do they think?

At least they'll think that gallery is a lesser gallery, as indeed it may be.
They'll also think you do not enforce your own standards.
Or perhaps you are not aware of the breach!
It's also likely they'll wonder why you have works there at all.

This can start to erode confidence in the value of your works.
Many leading artists won't show works in what they see as lesser outlets.
That is not just because they get few fewer sales.
It's mainly to preserve the perceived value of all works.

Works for sale in lesser outlets will tend to reduce value in better ones.
Conversely this could increase value in lesser outlets if clients are aware!
Galleries insist you not show in lesser outlets to preserve their own value!
Where would you rather sell at, a better outlet or a lesser one?
It's your choice - give them a pair of gloves.

What are the implications?
Take a great deal of care just what works you place where.
A lesser outlet can be very good for selling lesser works (if you do them).
They can sell works hard to move elsewhere (reduce prices considerably).
They become your wholesale outlet where you focus on turning over stock.
Recover something rather than getting the best price.
You can use auctions this way too.

Even this strategy needs to be handled carefully.
Some better galleries will object to this as well!
In the end the best outlets are valuable and worth keeping.

Do you produce works of variable quality and place them all on sale?
That's an even more dramatic illustration of not preserving your value.
Do **NOT** paint lesser works!
If so, do not sell them, give them away, or anything else - just destroy them!
They come back to haunt you like unwanted ghosts in the future, if you don't.

5. The strategy is price change.

Every marketer grossly underestimates the elasticity of price.
Most artists don't even know what it means!
They neglect prospects who'll cheerfully buy a higher priced premium option.
Of what they sell if it is offered to them.

You leave a lot of money on the table.
For example you could sell a leather bound folder with a suite of prints.
You could even sell entry to your studio via the blue door.
Then clients can walk through in the back instead of the red door in the front.

People will buy a premium option.
Most people don't understand how elastic price is (can vary).
Most people look at what everybody else in their business charges.
Then if they're really courageous they ask a little higher than the average.
Maybe they try to buy volume and are a little less than the average.

It's a very simple example you should put up on a wall where you see it.
How do you get a million dollar income in your art career?
Well you can get there with one transaction.
Provided you can sell somebody something for a million dollars.

But what if you're selling somebody something for $100?
You need to make 10,000 sales.
Making a million dollar sale is not 10,000 times harder than that!

But you won't do it by checking out the opposition.
That's not how you'll get there.
You need to be double or three times the best sold by opposition artists.
You could even be five times as much as some?
Then add some extras.

Price elasticity isn't really about the artwork.
It's about emotional reasons why they buy that particular work from you.

A number of increases in (say) 12 months could triple your income.
For example have clients pre-pay for works not yet even started!
Charge much more for this privilege.
But most artists underestimate it and most people don't understand it.

4. SELL FOR HIGH PRICES and MAKE MORE!

Reviewed by: Hufreesh Chopra - (Arizona, USA)

1. We've always been taught "You get what you pay for".
2. The psychology of price works in your favour.
3. What is quality?
4. Are quality and price linked?

1. We've always been taught "You get what you pay for".

Price sets up expectations.
PRICE IS a guide to **QUALITY**.

If you're struggling then a career turn around comes with higher prices.
If sales are hard to come by reducing prices is illogical.
Lower price means you must sell more to make the same return.
BUT high price means you can deliver more value too.
Ultimately the value you provide dictates profit you receive from prospects.

Increase the value and your income goes up.
High-profit products with high-margins give room to deliver sensational value.
You can throw in high-value extras.
And also afford to deliver truly unique unadvertised bonuses and follow-ups.
Your back-end products or services should be high value **AND** high priced!

You will OWN the marketplace if your work has a premium price:
Then you can afford to pay more to acquire a prospect.
But that prospect is a better prospect.
You compete against someone with $100 product and you a $10,000 work.
There's no contest, spend more on advertising, test unusual places.

You can even make bad results work for you.
A direct mailed high-priced product only needs a small % response.
A low-priced product requires a much bigger response to make money.

Most people undercharge for what they provide.
If your work isn't good enough to raise your price on it – make it better!
Making it cheaper will not work!

But you need people to sell to.
Where are the best prospects?
The foundation of an art career is your contact list.

Your contact list is the beginning of your recovery.
People who have bought in the past are the most likely to buy again.
Their friends and associates are the next most likely potential buyers.
The best source of new prospects is old clients.
They mainly arrive by what is commonly termed 'word of mouth' advertising.
Can you harness this powerful force?

2. Gain more sales by increasing the size of each transaction!

Charging more is one of the easiest ways to get more money.
Instead of new, exciting, and hard ways to get more money.
Here is a proven, easy way to get more money **RIGHT NOW** - charge more.

There is one main reason you should not be afraid to charge more.
People actually believe that if it costs more money it is better.
They want it just so they can have it and feel like they're special.
There's absolutely no difference between a Polo golf shirt and others.
Except the Polo label and the fact that it is more expensive.
But people think, "Oh, Polo is better," it's more expensive, that's why.

There is scientific research into links between wine prices and quality.
This research supports the notion that price determines quality.
Charging more will obviously help you increase the size of each transaction.
What if you're afraid to just charge more for the sake of charging more?
You could build more value into your product package.

What if you're selling a print?
Add an audio component and charge more for your advanced audio bundle.
Add screen cam video and charge more you've added value (video edition!)
Go from a print to the original painting and charge more.
An invitation to visit your studio is worth quite a bit for example.

Another thing you can do is add bonuses.
Then lift the price because the perceived value of your overall offer is better.
Another way you can charge more is add scarcity and exclusiveness.
Only allow 5 people to take your painting course and it's very expensive.
BUT those 5 people are going to get more personal interaction with you.
Instant price justification!

Another way to increase transaction value is to have a deluxe version.
Have a regular version and a deluxe version.
The deluxe version could be simply a piece of paper with the word "deluxe".
People would buy it ...just because it exists.
Obviously you should provide more value than that, but get the point.
If you paint in standard sizes (you should) then offer a standard basic frame.
The deluxe version has a better frame which has a label with the title on it.

3. What is quality?

Everyone thinks they can tell a high quality product from low quality.
But in reality things are not always so obvious.
Does a Rolex watch keep better time than a Seiko - are you sure?
Does a Mercedes have fewer mechanical problems than a Kia - certain?
Does a Montblanc pen write better than a Bic?
Does Coke taste better than Pepsi?
Is your painting better than mine?

More importantly is there any correlation between quality and sales?
If Coke outsells Pepsi then it must be a better quality cola?
Is that true and how do you know?
Quality is an idea that is widespread and sincerely believed in.
The way to a better (whatever) is to develop a better quality product.
But is this always so?
Building a product on the idea of quality is like building a house on sand.
But sand shifts!
You can build whatever idea of quality you might have into your artwork.
But that has little to do with your success in the marketplace.

Consumer magazines use objective measures to rank items on quality.
But these have little correlation with sales success.
The tests might actually show quality does not translate into sales.

Shopping for almost anything you look for a quality product or service.
If the price is right it's good value and you're likely to buy if you have money.
People buying paintings are no different.

But where does the idea of quality actually exist?
It's an idea in the consumer's mind and not in the product or service at all!
So it's actually a perception.
A quality product is about building this perception in the prospect's mind.
Tiffany did it with their packaging.

Narrow your focus and it is easier to build the quality idea.
You are a specialist (portrait artist, whatever) rather than a generalist.
A specialist is perceived to know more and be worth more than a generalist.
Does a heart surgeon know more than a general practitioner, many think so?
Is a portrait artist more skilled than a painter of a wide range of subjects?
What if they also used a variety of media?
A narrow focus is better if you wish to develop a quality image.

A key factors in building a high quality perception is a high price.
Rolex, Rolls-Royce, Montblanc, Chivas Regal, Jack Daniels are high priced.
High price is a benefit to clients too.
Affluent client gains satisfaction is by buying and consuming.
A Rolls-Royce is bought so people will notice it.
If a Rolls-Royce looked very similar to a Ford would it be as desirable?
Imagine someone in a restaurant has just ordered a $120 bottle of wine.
Would they want to know they can buy a $25 bottle that tastes just as good?
Would they be interested even if they thought that was actually so?

To promote your works with a quality image you need a higher price.
I mean considerably higher than otherwise similar works by other artists.
Decide what you can add to your brand (your works) to justify a higher price.
Rolex made its watches bigger and heavier with a unique wrist band.
Callaway golf clubs made drivers oversized and Montblanc pens are fatter.
Chivas Regal lets its Scotch whiskey age longer (12 years instead of 8).

What are you going to do to build a quality image for your artworks?
Narrow the focus; consider a better name for your product or service.
Add something distinctive and sell at a higher price.

4. Are quality and price linked?

There has been scientific research about such a link.
The research was into possible links between wine quality and price.
This was reported by Reuters in a wide variety of media.
14th January 2008 in the Proceedings of the National Academy of Sciences.
The reports were usually associated with sensationalist headlines.
BUT a synthesis of several of them is as follows:

Do higher wine prices boost drinking pleasure?
Researchers in California found increases of a person's enjoyment of wine.
All they had to do was stick a higher price on it.
CIT Professor of Economics, Antonio Rangel led a team.

They tested how marketing shapes consumers' perceptions.
AND whether it also enhances their enjoyment of the product.
21 volunteers sampled five different bottles of Cabernet Sauvignon.
They then rated their taste preferences.
The taste test was run 15 times, with wines presented in random order.

The taste test was blind except for information on the price of the wine.
Without telling volunteers, the researchers presented two of the wines twice.
Once with the true price tag and again with a fake one.
A $90 bottle of Cabernet Sauvignon was $10 and a $5 bottle was worth $45.

The researchers collected the test subjects' impressions of the wines.
Scans of brains to monitor neural activity in the medial orbito-frontal cortex.
Expected quality should trigger activity in the brain area that shows pleasure.

Researchers found:
People expect wines that cost more to be of higher quality.
They believe those wines are a more pleasurable than less expensive ones.

The test subjects sampled the same wine at different prices.
Pleasure was experienced at significantly higher levels when wine cost more.
The part of the brain responsible for pleasure also showed significant activity.
Inflating price on a bottle of wine enhanced drinking experience.
This was even when the part of the brain that interprets taste wasn't affected.

Volunteers consistently gave higher ratings to more "expensive" wines.
Brain scans also showed greater neural activity in the pleasure centre.
When sampling the higher priced wines.
This indicated the increased pleasure reported was a real effect in the brain.

In other words the more wine costs, the more people enjoy it.
It doesn't matter how it really tastes.
Many studies have looked at how marketing affects behaviour.
This is the first to show that it has a direct effect on the brain.

Scientists and economists believe quality of experience depends on:
The properties of the product and the state of the consumer - if thirsty or not.
But this study shows the brain's rewards centre takes into account:
Subjective beliefs about the quality of the experience.
If you believe that the experience is better, even though it's the same wine.
The rewards centre of the brain encodes it as feeling better.
Thus people's beliefs about quality of wine affects taste for the brain.

It is likely price is just one factor that influences the tasting experience.
The study reported, only investigated the influence of price.
Study showed the brain's reward-centre taking into account subjective belief.
Then other subjective factors are likely to have a similar influence.
People's beliefs about the quality of wine affect how it tastes for the brain.
People believe expert wine ratings, knowledge influences tasting experience.

If an experience is pleasurable, the brain uses it to guide future choice.
A conclusion with implications for marketing influencing perception of quality.
Strategies as expert ratings, peer reviews, information on country of origin,
store and brand names and repeated exposure to advertisements are a part.

Marketers have not been waiting for research results.
They have assumed these latest results to be true for a long time.
Prestige brands are marketed as finding support and resist price reduction.
Those that have had price reductions found their prestige image eroded.

Marketing obviously affects behaviour.
This is self-evident for otherwise there is no point in marketing.
Marketing is meant to influence behaviour.
The reported research supports what actually happens in the marketplace.
The research is no different for those trading on price as quality is irrelevant.

If an experience is pleasurable, the brain uses it to guide future choice.
Important implications for marketing aiming to influence quality perceptions.
The brain pleasure centre is influenced by tasting experience linked to price.
A similar influence where a visual experience is linked to price is probable.
That has equally important implications for marketing artworks.

Similar research in relation to artworks would produce similar results.
The more a painting costs, the more people assume it is a quality work.
This would be regardless of what it really looks like.
Have you witnessed that actually happen?

Remember van Gogh - when he was alive they couldn't find a buyer.
These days they are the top of the prestige tree.
The works themselves haven't changed for they are still the same as always.

What has changed has been the perception of value of those works.
This perception of value is in people's minds due to prices now obtained.
The viewing experience has been influenced by art historians and critics.
They are themselves influenced by current price levels.

There are common beliefs among artists.
The quality of the experience depends on the properties of the product.
Such assertions must now be in serious doubt.

Is there any such thing as good art?
What exactly is quality when applied to art works?
Is this any different from wine quality?

How does this influence the marketing of your own works?

5. WRAPPING UP!

Reviewed by Sanya Lechito – (Lagos, Nigeria)
1. What should you have on price tags?
2. There's power in leverage!
3. What is the long term value of your clients?

1. What should you have on price tags?

Many galleries have labels, such as price tags on each work.
This supplies information about the work, its artist and how much it costs.
Most retailers do something similar and some are required by law to do so.
Keeping all this information up to date is not a big task, but it is never-ending.
Quite a few years ago my gallery used to do this too.
Then we started to notice the really big galleries did not.
I wondered why this was so for it certainly looked neater.
Our labels never stayed straight so I gave up and stopped putting labels on.

Then we noticed some things happening.
People started asking about the paintings.
Who did them, how much they were, etc.
Well I guess that's not so surprising is it?
People wanted the information we previously supplied in a written form.

As a result we could tell them lots of other things not on the label.
We could let them know when a next exhibition by the artist was scheduled.
We could ask the viewer if they'd like to be included on the mailing list.
We could say we had other larger, smaller, dearer or cheaper works in stock.

We were getting information we hadn't previously been able to obtain.
Now we knew which works people were interested in, before just which sold.
In the new situation if people asked about a painting there was interest.

If they ask the price, there's buying interest, this is useful information.
If an artist has works on show, about which there's regular price enquiries.
It's likely to sell eventually but if it doesn't the price is too high for our clients.

On the other hand if no-one asks about the price.
Whether it's too dear isn't a factor, there's something wrong with the image.
It was possible to give the artist with more meaningful feedback than before.

There was one group who don't like this idea at all.
It's those people who don't want to buy, but who are curious about the prices.
They usually ask why there are no labels but don't often ask the price.
Many are artists but I knew they weren't buyers so I didn't worry about them.

Retailers selling up-market goods generally do not have price-tags.
If works have price tags, you're selling on price even if you don't want to.
There's no chance to say why they are excellent value, whatever the price.
So we found out why big galleries don't have price tags on their paintings.
It's neater, but more importantly each client is engaged in a conversation.
It's more professional and there's a better chance of selling the works.
Some galleries don't publish price in catalogues, an extension of the idea.

So it was better not to have any information displayed with the works.
Visitors are used to and expect it, but doesn't mean it's what you do.
At exhibitions work was numbered so people looked at the catalogue.
However I didn't always have the price in the catalogue.
Works not in an exhibition never had anything, not even a catalogue.

Sometimes I had several catalogues with different prices.
At an exhibition I could be more flexible with pricing.
Prior to the opening there were lower prices than at the opening and after.
This encouraged early buying by giving a lower price during the pre-opening.
It was an incentive so we could start an exhibition with many sales made.
That price was the one the artist wanted, so they didn't lose anything.

We tried to sell most works before an exhibition opened.
That happened so we were ahead due to increased number of earlier sales!
The exhibition price (usually plus 10%) was to start educating people.
They were now exposed to the new standard price for this artist's works.
The new catalogue reinforced this new price structure.

However not having anything with the works is an excellent idea too.
If people are art lovers they can look at the paintings and just enjoy them.
Anyone who thinks they might like to own one has to ask the price.
Now you can get straight into a sales discussion (ask questions).
You have identified potential buyers and which works they are interested in.
Usually you never find this out until they buy.
That means now you can follow up with more certainty than previously.
You can guide the conversation from thinking they might buy to buying.

Not having tags was one of the best strategies I used in my gallery.
Basically it's the best way to get into a conversation with gallery visitors.
You can ask questions when they start talking to you.
It's not just more personal for the visitor, it's more professional too.

People assume works are expensive for there are no visible prices.
That's not a bad thing.
A variation might be to have **NO** images or prices on your website.
A website could have details of paintings available (subject, size, medium)
BUT with **NO** image or price.
This is cheap to do (no images) you supply details but take less space.
It could trigger prospect imagination and lead to a sale.
Supply details on how enquiries are made (visit gallery, studio, whatever).

2. There's power in leverage!

A lever applied in a certain situation provides magnification of effort.
Crowbars are used this way, but screwdrivers are also levers for twisting.
Levers aren't just mechanical, they can be any tool used to magnify effort.
Levers make the seemingly impossible happen, in business this is leverage.

Let's say you focus on local subjects for your art.
As you paint mainly local landscapes you depend on local buyers or tourists.
You place ads in the local paper every Saturday to entice these buyers.
You can calculate exactly the cost of each sale.
Divide the annual cost of newspaper ads by the number of sales made.
You can even calculate exactly the cost of each visitor.
Divide the annual cost to the newspaper by the number of visitors in a year.
You need to keep records of sales and visitors, but that's not difficult.

The cost of an ad is $100 and 50 paintings are sold in a year.
The advertising cost per sale is $104 ($100x52 divided by 50).
The cost per visitor, if 20 people visit a gallery or studio each week is $10.

How could leverage be applied in this situation?
Most tourists will tend to visit a tourist information facility.
There they find out where galleries and artists might be located.
The above newspaper spending has not attracted any of these people.
Yet they are included in the figures (20 per weekend).
So the newspaper is only attracting local people.

Therefore the real cost is much higher than my calculations show.
Let's say 6 out of the 20 people per weekend are tourists.
The cost per local visitor is now $14.29.
Perhaps not too much, but 43% more than previously thought.
Perhaps only one tourist in every 10 buys a painting.
This alters the cost per sale to local people from advertising to $115.55.

None of this is leverage, just calculations to show the present scenario.
Use a different strategy to find another way to attract more people.
That's leverage if it costs less money.
It's better leverage if you find a way to more sales for fewer visitor numbers.
So look for other ways to spend $5200 or less, and still achieve the above.
$50 in cash could be given to anyone introducing someone who buys a work.
This could include themselves.
What if you eliminate the newspaper advertising?
If the same quantity of work is sold to local people, you are $3409 better off.

There may or may not be more visitors but it's sales that matter.
The people claiming the $50 are levers helping you sell paintings.
Think on these lines and you can develop sophisticated leverage strategies.

Sales and direct marketing tools can bring forward buying decisions.
Assumption is a marketing target does intend to buy it's just a matter of time.
A prospect declines to buy if a sales attempt is made when they aren't ready.
This doesn't mean they wouldn't be ready at a later time though.
That's why much general advertising contains bait.
Buy now and you'll also receive these fantastic steak knives.
The steak knives are bait to bring a purchase decision forward (buy now).

You could offer a discount if a client buys before your exhibition opens.
Buy this (painting, art class) on your condition (at this time, from this stock).
And you'll receive this extra (discount, steak knives, a print, box of cards).
Construct an offer so there is a benefit to you over and above making a sale.
For example clear old stock, or your exhibition kicks off with many red dots.
None of this is effective without linking it to your database.

3. What is the long term value of your clients?

Segmenting clients allows you to see different patterns of behaviour.
Thinking beyond a single sale it becomes possible to project into the future.
It may also mean we can consider a single sale in a different light.
One aspect you should consider is the long term value of a client.
Who has spent most, how frequently and at what average price?

You've segmented your clients and have done so for a number of years.
In this case you should be able to calculate the average $value of a sale.
Just the total $ spent by clients divided by the sales in a specific period.
We'll call this amount $X.
You could also calculate the average sales for a typical client.
Total sales divided by the number of clients over the time (say 4 years) = Y.

The long term value of a typical client will be $X x Y.
An average sale is $1450 ($X).
An average number of sales is 7 per client (Y).
The long term value (4 years say) of a typical client is then $10,150 ($X x Y).
Obviously some clients will spend more than this and others less.

If you realize the long term value of a client you may spend more.
It pays off if your figures are accurate and you make a profit in the long run.
You need to keep the necessary figures for a period of time.
Then calculations are reasonably accurate but initially you have to guess.

Also calculate the value of a specific client over the same period.
Identify clients who are returning above the average and those who are not.
Try to upgrade the latter group, and certainly nurture the former clients.
If you are successful then the averages will change, for the better.
Contact lists let you to maintain and develop a relationship with each client.
That continues over the years necessary for long-term value to be realized.

WHERE NEXT:

BUT being a professional artist is NOW harder than it ever was.
There are other books that link with this book.
You might need one or more of them:

PLANNING - Means success.
http://www.amazon.com/dp/B087SCD1NY

CAREER BASICS - Planning.
http://www.amazon.com/dp/B087SCJYX3

FINDING BUYERS - How?
http://www.amazon.com/dp/B087SM58GJ

FIRST WEBSITE - Simple is best.
http://www.amazon.com/dp/B087SFZ6RD

SUCCESSFUL SELLING - Learn how.
http://www.amazon.com/dp/B087SHDKPN

FRAMING = helps sales
http://www.amazon.com/dp/B087SGS6MB

CHRISTMAS - Special approaches.
http://www.amazon.com/dp/B087SHDKPN

TAKE THE PLUNGE - become professional
http://www.amazon.com/dp/B087SFTD61

PRODUCTIVITY – the foundation
http://www.amazon.com/dp/B087S87HLD

COPYRIGHT - making money from copyright sales.
http://www.amazon.com/dp/B0892HWYTV

NOT NOW:

Perhaps one of these books could interest you then?

Write about your own memories.
http://www.amazon.com/dp/B087DWKPTP

A simple way to start developing creativity.
If you are a parent, teacher or someone who meets a group regularly?
http://www.amazon.com/dp/B088T1KFQZ

Here is how most people start becoming an artist!
http://www.amazon.com/dp/B088Y1DPL6

More of my memories.
http://www.amazon.com/dp/B088Y4RPL9

Start an art career but it's NOW is harder than it ever was.
http://www.amazon.com/dp/B088T7VJ76

SEND TO:

Know anyone interested in chocolate recipes?
Then send them this link.
http://www.amazon.com/dp/B088Y4RPL9

Know anyone interested in THIS book?
http://www.amazon.com/dp/B087S85HS8

www.ingramcontent.com/pod-product-compliance
Lightning Source LLC
Chambersburg PA
CBHW030531220526
45463CB00007B/2781